ANIMALS EATING

How Animals Chomp, Chew, Slurp and Swallow

WRITTEN BY PAMELA HICKMAN

ILLUSTRATED BY PAT STEPHENS

Kids Can Press

Thanks to Pat Stephens, Marie Bartholomew, Laura Ellis and Laurie Wark
for another great team effort in this series. Thanks also to veterinarians Mark and Karen Smith
of the Cornwallis Veterinarian Clinic for their help with specific research
and to Angela, Connie and Jenny for test-driving the activities.

Kids Can Press acknowledges the financial support of the Ontario Arts Council, the Canada Council for the Arts and the Government of Canada, through the BPIDP, for our publishing activity.

Published in Canada by
Kids Can Press Ltd.
29 Birch Avenue
Toronto, ON M4V 1E2

Published in the U.S. by
Kids Can Press Ltd.
2250 Military Road
Tonawanda, NY 14150

Edited by Laurie Wark
Designed by Marie Bartholomew
Printed and bound in Hong Kong by
Book Art Inc., Toronto

The hardcover edition of this book is smyth sewn casebound.

The paperback edition of this book is limp sewn with a drawn-on cover.

CM 01 0 9 8 7 6 5 4 3 2 1
CM PA 01 0 9 8 7 6 5 4 3 2 1

Canadian Cataloguing in Publication Data

Hickman, Pamela
   Animals eating : how animals chomp, chew, slurp and swallow

ISBN 1-55074-577-8 (bound)   ISBN 1-55074-579-4 (pbk.)

1. Animals — Food — Juvenile literature. I. Stephens, Pat. II. Title.

QL756.5.H52 2001   j591.5'3   C00-931431-8

Kids Can Press is a Nelvana company

Contents

Introduction

Imagine eating a big meal and then not eating again for a year. That's what an anaconda does. What if you lived in the desert and never had a drink of water, like a kangaroo rat? Or you might live entirely on liquids, the way a vampire bat does. And what if you caught your food with your tongue like a chameleon can, or used your eyeballs to help you swallow, the way a toad does? In this book you'll discover many more weird and wonderful ways that animals eat and drink.

Most animals are adapted to eat either plants or other animals. Some eat only one kind of food, while others can feed on different things. When a plant is eaten by an animal, and then that animal is eaten by another animal, a food chain is created. All plants and animals are part of many food chains in nature. In a balanced environment, there are enough plants to feed the plant eaters and enough animals to feed the meat eaters.

Turn the page to find out more about food chains. Then read on to meet some amazing animals and compare their eating habits with yours. Visit a watering hole on the African plains to see how different animals drink. Try some of the activities and experiments and learn what an animal eats by looking at its teeth, see how a bird's gizzard works, discover what it would be like to eat the way a fly does and much more.

Chameleon

Making connections

Nature is like a giant buffet table, with something for every creature to eat. The herbivores eat plants, the carnivores eat meat, the omnivores eat plants and meat, and the scavengers eat the leftovers. There is no waste. Each plant and animal is part of a food chain that connects it with other creatures. For instance, a mouse may nibble on some seeds, a snake may swallow the mouse and an owl may catch the snake. Each food chain begins with a plant. Since animals often eat more than one thing, many food chains overlap and are sometimes called a food web.

Who eats what

- bee flies and male mosquitoes feed on flowers
- female mosquitoes feed on warm-blooded animals such as birds and moose
- moose eat plants
- dragonflies eat mosquitoes
- frogs eat insects
- herons eat frogs and fish
- fish eat frogs and insects
- ospreys eat fish

Osprey

Male mosquito

Heron

Female mosquito

Moose

Bee fly

Dragonfly

Water lily

Fish

Frog

Arrowhead

Pickerel weed

Follow the food

With some help from an adult, make a model
of the food web in this marsh.

You'll need:

a piece of wood
about 25 cm x 40 cm
(10 in. x 15 in.)
and at least 1 cm
(1/2 in.) thick

paint and a
paintbrush
(optional)

a fine-tipped
marker that can
write on wood

4 cm (1 1/2 in.)
flat-head nails

a hammer

several different
colors of yarn

scissors

1. Paint the wood to look like a marsh, if you wish. Write names of plants and animals so that they are spread out over the board in roughly the same positions as in the picture on page 6.

2. Hammer a nail beside each name. Leave the nails sticking up about 2.5 cm (1 in.).

3. Tie the end of the yarn to the nail beside a plant name. Unravel the yarn until you reach a nail next to an animal that would eat that plant (see "Who eats what" on page 6). Wrap the yarn around the nail then connect the yarn to another animal that could come next in the food chain. Continue until you reach the end of the food chain. Tie the yarn tightly in a knot around the last nail and then cut it.

4. With another color of yarn, follow a new food chain from nail to nail. You may start with the same plant or a different plant. Use a different color of yarn for each new food chain you make. Food chains can overlap where one animal eats more than one thing. In a real marsh, there are many more creatures and hundreds of food connections.

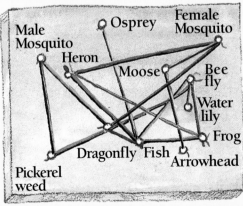

Marvelous mouths

The mouth is the first stop that food makes on its way through an animal's body. Mouths come in many shapes and sizes, and most mouths are adapted to the kind of food that an animal eats. Some insect eaters have extra-long tongues for catching and pulling in their prey. A snake's special jaws can open wide enough to swallow food that is larger than the snake's own head. And meat eaters are well equipped with sharp teeth for killing and tearing up their food.

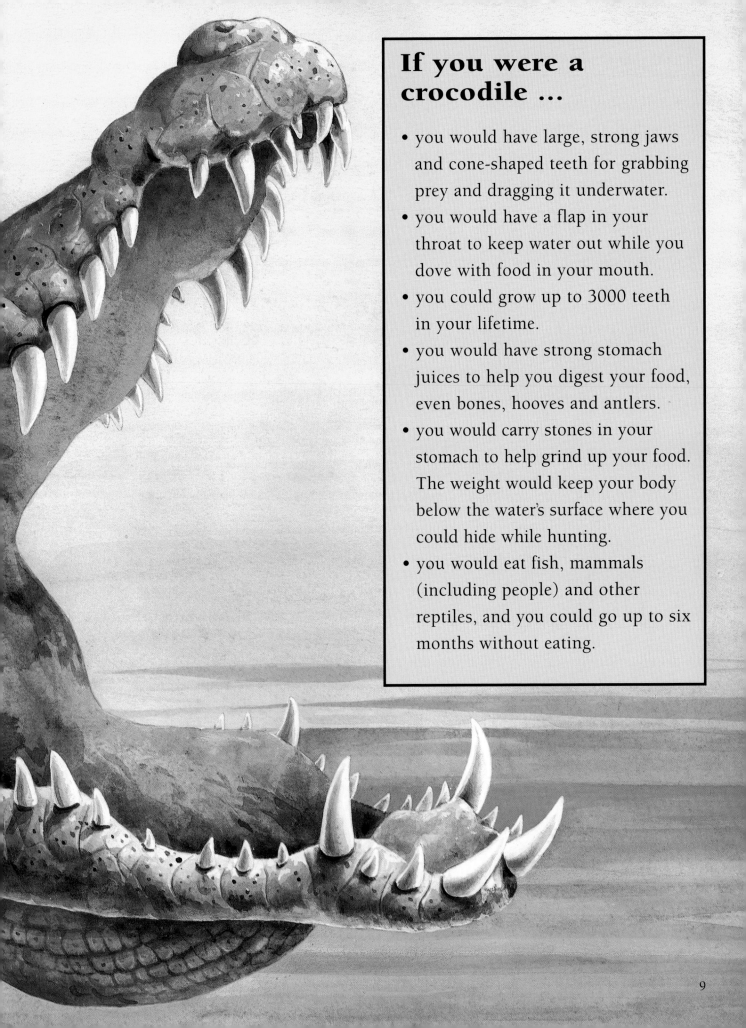

If you were a crocodile ...

- you would have large, strong jaws and cone-shaped teeth for grabbing prey and dragging it underwater.
- you would have a flap in your throat to keep water out while you dove with food in your mouth.
- you could grow up to 3000 teeth in your lifetime.
- you would have strong stomach juices to help you digest your food, even bones, hooves and antlers.
- you would carry stones in your stomach to help grind up your food. The weight would keep your body below the water's surface where you could hide while hunting.
- you would eat fish, mammals (including people) and other reptiles, and you could go up to six months without eating.

Tongue-tied

How far can you stick out your tongue? Imagine if it stretched the length of your body, the way a chameleon's does. A chameleon's tube-shaped tongue is hollow and fits folded up over a long, bony support inside its mouth. When a chameleon sees an insect, muscles in the reptile's tongue, jaws and neck make the tongue shoot forward. A sticky pad on the tip of its tongue helps the lizard catch and hold its prey. A chameleon's tongue can catch and retrieve an insect faster than you can blink! Here are some more amazing kinds of tongues.

Toad

If you were a toad, your tongue would be attached at the front of your mouth instead of at the back. When a toad sees a fly approaching, it flips its tongue forward and out of its mouth. A sticky pad on the end of its tongue traps the fly.

A hairy woodpecker snakes its tongue through insect tunnels inside of rotting trees. Its sticky tongue has a hard tip and tiny hooked hairs to spear the ants and beetles it finds.

Hairy woodpecker

An anteater's tiny mouth is just big enough for its sticky, wormlike tongue to shoot in and out, catching up to 30 000 ants and termites in a day. South America's giant anteater's tongue is more than twice as long as this page!

Anteater

Tongue trapper

Make this frog tongue model and see how good your aim is.

You'll need:

a thick rubber band or piece of elastic about 10 cm (4 in.) long

scissors

a paint stir stick or similar-sized piece of wood

a thumbtack

a hammer

a stapler

a piece of Velcro, (hooked and nonhooked sides), about 2.5 cm (1 in.) long

a piece of felt, about 5 cm x 5 cm (2 in. x 2 in.)

1. Cut the rubber band and tack one end of it to an end of the stir stick so that it lays flat along the stick.

2. Staple a 1 cm x 2 cm (1/2 in. x 3/4 in.) piece of hooked Velcro on top of the loose end of the rubber band.

3. Staple the nonhooked piece of Velcro to the felt and place it on a table.

4. Lay the stick, tacked end forward, flat on the table aimed at the felt. Hold the stick in place with one hand. With the other hand, gently pull back on the rubber band and then let go. You may have to adjust the position of your stick and try again before you get the right aim and speed.

5. The rubber band is like a frog's tongue as it shoots forward out of its mouth. The Velcro on the end is the sticky pad that the frog uses to catch insects. When the hooked Velcro hits the felt or the nonhooked Velcro, it will stick the way a frog's tongue sticks to an insect.

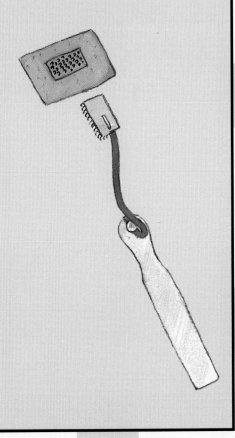

Baleen banquet

Animals have all different kinds of teeth adapted to the food they eat. Instead of having teeth, this blue whale has stiff, black plates of horn called baleen hanging from the roof of its mouth. When the whale feeds, it opens up its mouth and sucks in ocean water containing tiny animals. The whale then closes its mouth and raises its enormous tongue to force the water back out through the baleen. The baleen works like a sieve, trapping food inside the whale's mouth. The whale's tongue scrapes the baleen clean and the animal swallows the food.

If you were a blue whale ...

- you would weigh more than two tons when you were born.
- you would drink more than 200 L (50 gal.) of your mother's milk per day when you were a baby and you would gain 90 kg (200 lb.) a day.
- you would have baleen instead of teeth. As an adult, each day you would eat up to 6 to 8 tons of krill, a tiny shrimplike creature.
- you would grow to be longer than a basketball court and four times heavier than the largest known dinosaur.

Teeth talk

Look in a mirror and open your mouth up wide. Check out the different shapes of teeth in your mouth and try to figure out what they are best designed to do.

When you eat, you have four different kinds of teeth at work. Your front teeth, or incisors, cut and bite. Your canines rip up tough food. Your premolars and molars grind and chew.

Other mammals have the same kinds of teeth, but their teeth may be specially adapted for eating specific kinds of food. For instance, cougars and other big carnivores have extra large canines for stabbing prey. Their premolars, called carnassials, have very sharp edges that cut like scissors. Sheep, which eat plants, have very small incisors and canines. They have large, flat premolars and molars for grinding up plants. Rodents, such as beavers, have no canines at all. They are best known for their four large incisors, which are perfect for gnawing. A rodent's incisors never stop growing and are continually chiseled down to a sharp edge as the animal eats.

In some animals, special teeth have developed into things that don't really look like teeth anymore. An elephant's tusks are actually its incisors and a walrus's tusks are canines. These specialized teeth are used for feeding as well as defense.

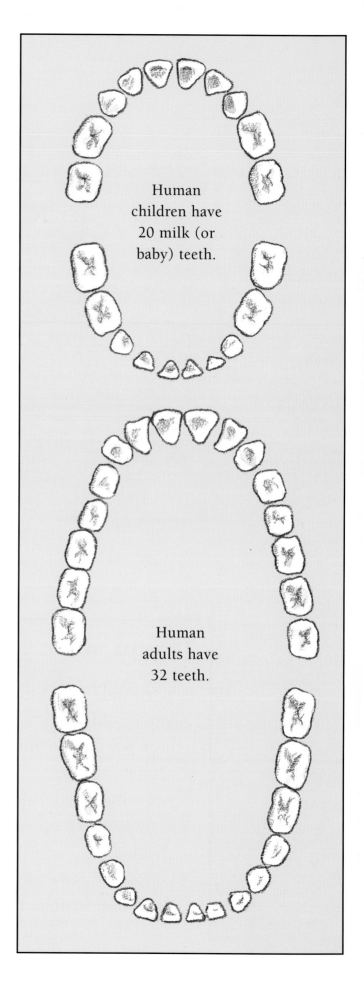

Human children have 20 milk (or baby) teeth.

Human adults have 32 teeth.

Straight from the horse's mouth

If you want to know how old a horse is, look in its mouth. The best way to discover a horse's age is by studying its teeth. The shape of a horse's incisors changes with time. Also, the older the horse, the longer and more angled its front teeth are. Sometimes the expression "long in the tooth" is used to describe a person who is old.

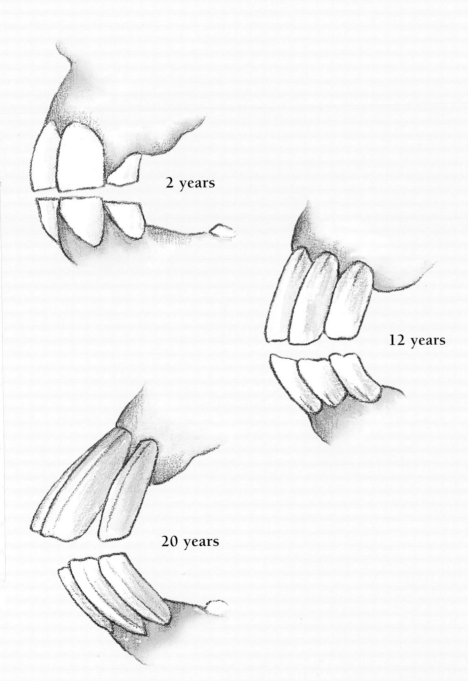

2 years

12 years

20 years

Tell the tooth

Can you match these teeth with their owners?

A. rodent (porcupine)
B. herbivore (deer)
C. carnivore (wolf)
D. omnivore (human)

1.
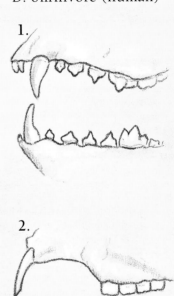

2.

3.
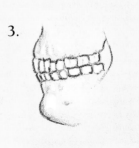

4.
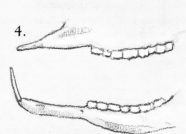

Turn to page 40 for the answers.

15

Pass the plants, please

Every plant on Earth is food for some creature, from the tiniest insect to the biggest elephant. Many plants are eaten by more than one animal. For example, a rabbit may nibble the leaves of a plant while an insect feeds on its roots, and a hummingbird laps up nectar from a flower while a mouse chews on its seeds. Animals that eat only plants are called herbivores. Many plant eaters have special adaptations that help them harvest and digest their food. Some herbivores, called ruminants, have to chew the same food over and over again until it can be digested. And some animals are so specialized they can eat only one kind of plant. Now look up, way up, to find out what is special about this giraffe.

If you were a giraffe ...

- you would be the tallest animal on Earth.
- your long legs and neck would help you reach food that other animals couldn't get to.
- your long, flexible tongue would wrap around the leaves and shoots at the top of acacia trees and pull them into your mouth.
- your tongue would be covered by a natural sunscreen to protect it from the hot sun.

Snacking on seeds

All flowering plants make seeds and provide food for many hungry animals. If you have a birdfeeder, you've probably noticed different birds eating the seeds that you put out. Each kind of bird feeds in its own way. A blue jay traps a large seed under its toes and hammers at it with its long, pointed beak until the seed breaks open. A grosbeak uses its thick, sharp bill to crush seeds in its mouth. The small nuthatch wedges a seed into a groove in the tree bark. Then it bangs away at the seed with its narrow, pointy beak until the seed cracks open. Crossbills have sharp, curved beaks with crossed tips. This unique shape is perfect for prying seeds out of cones.

To help a bird digest its crunchy meal, it has a thick-walled, muscular gizzard attached to its stomach. Grains of sand and tiny stones inside the gizzard help grind up the food. In order to gather seeds and carry them away, a bird has a pouch in its throat called a crop.

Blue jay

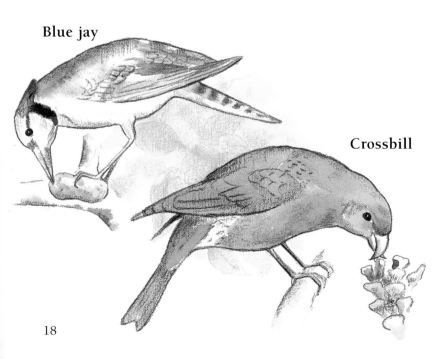

Crossbill

Cheeky

Rodents, such as the European hamster, have huge cheek pouches so that they can carry seeds to their burrows for winter storage. Large cheeks are useful in other ways, too. If attacked, a hamster will blow its load of seeds in the face of its enemy, giving the rodent enough time to escape. Some hamsters even fill their cheeks with air to help them stay afloat in water.

How a gizzard works

Try this experiment to see how gizzards help birds grind up the seeds they eat.

1. Place the gravel and the birdseed in the center of the fabric.

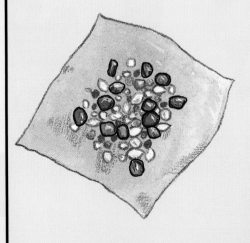

2. Gather the fabric around the gravel and birdseed to make a small pouch. Secure the fabric tightly with the rubber band. This pouch represents the bird's gizzard.

3. With your fingers, mash and grind the contents of the pouch together for about five minutes. Your fingers are working like the muscles in the walls of a gizzard.

4. Open the pouch. How do the seeds look? You should find that they are ground up into smaller pieces. Once a bird's gizzard has worked on the food, it passes into the intestines, where special juices help to digest the food even more.

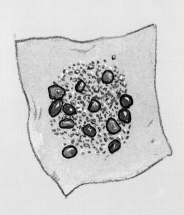

Eating again

Are you a chewer or a gulper at mealtime? Ruminants, such as bison, cows, deer and sheep, hardly chew their food at all before they swallow it down. They are so busy eating that they don't have time to chew. Instead of having just one stomach like people do, ruminants have up to four stomachs. When the animal swallows grass and other plants, the food goes to the first two stomachs, where it is mushed up into a pulp by bacteria. Later in the day when the animal is resting, the pulp — called cud — is sent back to the mouth to be chewed again. Finally, the cud is swallowed and sent to the third and fourth stomachs, where it is totally broken down by strong stomach juices. It takes about 24 hours for a ruminant to digest grass, but rougher food, such as bark, can take up to seven days!

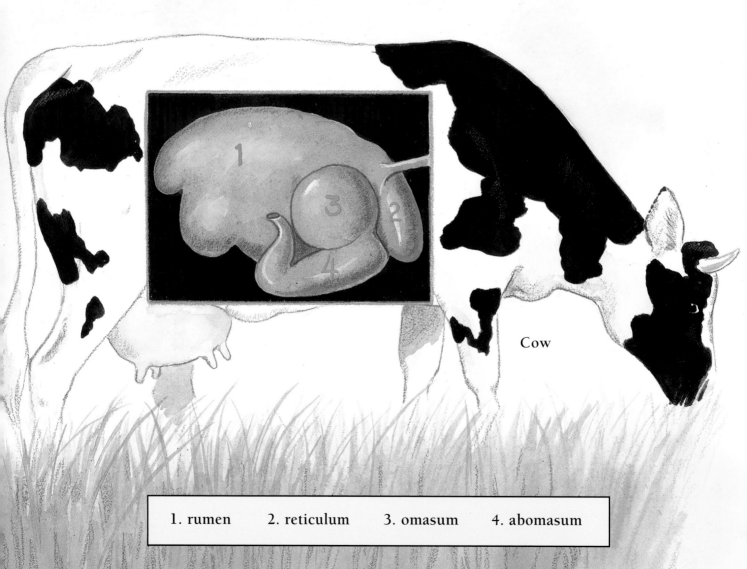

Cow

1. rumen   2. reticulum   3. omasum   4. abomasum

The bison is the largest land animal in North America. It is a ruminant with a four-chambered stomach and it grazes on grass all year round. It uses its large, flat nose as a snowplough to uncover grass during the winter.

21

Picky eaters

If you ate only one kind of food and something destroyed your entire food supply, what would happen? You would either have to change your eating habits and start feeding on something else, or you would die. Unfortunately, some animals can't switch to another food. When an animal's habitat is destroyed and its food is no longer available, it becomes endangered. The caterpillar of the Karner blue butterfly eats only wild lupine. When the habitat of the wild lupine in southern Ontario, Canada, was destroyed by construction and agriculture, the Karner blue butterflies that lived there disappeared. Here are two other animals that eat only one kind of food. They could become extinct if their food source is destroyed.

Giant panda

The giant panda of China depends on bamboo shoots for food.

Koala

The Australian koala eats only
eucalyptus leaves.

You are what you eat

If you were a honey bee, your
whole future would depend on
what you were fed after you
hatched. During the first three days
of their lives, all bee grubs are fed
special food called royal jelly to
help them grow quickly. During the
next three days, only future queen
bees continue to get royal jelly. All
the others are fed a mixture of
honey and pollen called beebread.
These grubs grow up to be the
workers for the hive.

Honey bee

Meat on the menu

There are no grocery stores for wildlife. Meat-eating animals, called carnivores, have to spend most of their days looking for prey and trying to kill it. Many predators have keen senses of eyesight, hearing and smell to help them find prey. They also come equipped with strong jaws, sharp teeth or beaks, and powerful claws for killing and tearing apart their food. The plan of attack is different for each predator. Some animals, such as snakes, sneak up on their prey. Wolves use the whole pack to stalk and chase a victim, but mink hunt alone. Carnivores feed on the prey that is easiest to catch; usually the slowest, weakest, youngest or oldest.

If you were a longtail weasel ...

- you would have a keen sense of smell for hunting.
- your strong jaws and sharp canine teeth would help you kill and hold onto mice, voles, squirrels, birds, rabbits and large insects.
- you would eat half your body weight in food each day.
- you would store extra food in your burrow for the winter. You would spray the stored food with your musk scent to keep other animals away.
- your brown coat would turn white for winter in the north. You would blend in with the snow so that you could sneak up on your prey.
- your long, slender body would be able to move quickly and easily through the underground burrows of prey.

Open wide

You may be able to fit a plum into your mouth without cutting it up, but a watermelon would never fit. People need to cut up or bite off pieces of food before eating them. Snakes can eat large prey whole without a problem. Here's how they do it.

Put your finger on your cheek, close to the top of your ear. Now open your mouth as wide as it will go. You should feel your lower jaw move where it is hinged to your upper jaw. Your mouth won't open any wider because of the hinge. Snakes also have a hinged joint where their upper and lower jaws meet, but a snake can unhinge its jaws and drop its lower jaw all the way open. This lets a snake put its mouth around something even bigger than its own head.

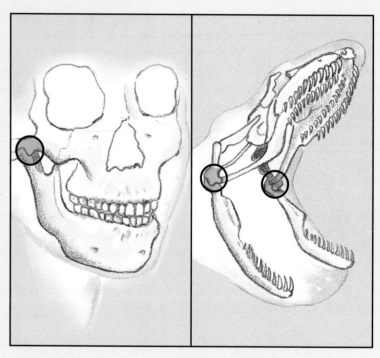

Human jaws   **Snake jaws**

If you feel your chin, you will notice that your lower jaw is one solid bone. A snake's lower jaw is in two pieces and they are joined by an elastic tissue at the "chin." When a snake is eating, the two bones can be stretched apart so the snake can open its mouth even wider.

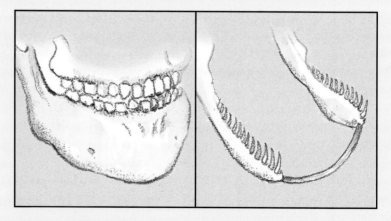

Human lower jaw   **Snake lower jaw**

Pythons and anacondas are the largest snakes in the world. They can capture and kill animals much larger than themselves. They coil their muscular bodies around the prey and squeeze until it suffocates. Once the prey is dead, the snakes stretch their jaws around the food and swallow it whole. A large meal like this takes many days to digest and these snakes may not need to eat again for a year.

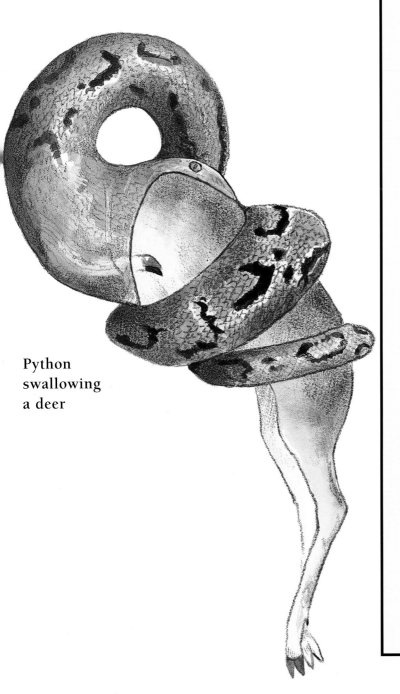

Python swallowing a deer

Fast food

Snakes can go a long time between meals, but you may eat three meals a day plus snacks. The more active you are, the more food your body needs to give you enough energy for your activities. Other animals, such as hummingbirds and shrews, must eat all the time to stay alive. Their bodies work harder and use up energy much more quickly than most animals. They have to eat constantly to supply the energy they need. The pygmy shrew of North America eats its own weight in food every three hours. If you had to match that, how many quarter-pound burgers would you need to eat in one day? Figure it out like this:

Your weight in pounds x 4 = number of burgers you would need every three hours (four quarter-pound burgers = one pound of food).

Number of burgers per three hours x 8 = number of burgers you would need per day.

Waste not, want not

Do you like leftovers? In nature, animals that eat the leftovers of another animal's meal are called scavengers. Vultures and other scavengers simply wait for something else to make a kill and then they move in for the remains.

If you drive down the road and see an animal that has been killed by a car, you may also see a group of birds, such as crows or gulls, busily feeding on the carcass. Although these birds feed on many different kinds of food, when they spot a dead animal, they quickly zero in for a meal. Turkey vultures, which range from southern Canada to South America, are specialists when it comes to cleaning up carcasses.

If you were a turkey vulture …

- you would feed mainly on dead animals, called carrion.
- you would have keen eyesight and an excellent sense of smell to help you find food from far off.
- you would use your long, hooked beak and sharp claws to tear the flesh off the dead animal.
- your strong digestive system would destroy the large amounts of bacteria in carrion, so you wouldn't get sick.
- you might eat so much at one time that you would become too heavy to fly. You would then have to wait until some of the food was digested before taking off.

Get in line

When you sit down to a meal, your family shares the food on the table. Wild animals that live together in families, such as wolves and lions, also share their food. When a kill is made, the head pair of wolves eats first, then the rest of the pack joins in. Although female lions usually kill the prey, the males eat first and the females and young wait their turn. If there is food left over, scavengers such as vultures or hyenas may come and finish off the carcass. Scientists used to think that hyenas always ate the leftovers from a lion's meal. New research shows that hyenas usually kill their own prey, and that lions sometimes take over food that was killed by hyenas.

Wolves

Blood brothers and sisters

Vampire bats roost together in large groups and seem to have a "buddy system" for sharing their food. Each bat needs to drink up to its own weight in blood each night, often from a cow or a horse. If a bat returns to its roost without finding a meal, another bat will spit up part of its blood meal and share it with the hungry bat. By sharing food, the bats help each other survive.

Whose hoard?

If you can't finish your sandwich at lunch, you might wrap it up and save it for later. Many wild animals save food, sometimes for months. They collect food when it is plentiful and hoard it for winter or the dry season, when food is scarce. Can you match the animal with its stored food? Turn to page 40 for the answers.

ANIMALS

Red squirrel

Mole

Honey bee

Honeypot ant

Leopard

Pika

STORED FOOD

Honeycomb

Earthworms

Storage ants

Antelope

Mini haystack of
collected grasses

Mushrooms

Quenching a thirst

All living things contain water and need it to survive. More than half your weight is from the water in your body. When you feel thirsty, it's your body's way of telling you that you need a refill. For many animals, having a drink means different things. For example, frogs and toads don't drink through their mouths. Instead, they soak up the water they need through their special skin. Australia's koalas never drink because they get all of the water they need from the eucalyptus leaves they eat. Desert animals are experts at conserving their body water. Many avoid the hot sun during the day and come out at night to feed when it is cooler and damper. The saguaro cactus of the southwestern United States and northern Mexico is not only a source of water for some animals, but it also provides a home for this tiny elf owl.

If you were an elf owl ...

- you would be one of the smallest owls in the world, only growing up to 15 cm (6 in.) high.
- you would spend the hot desert days sheltered in an abandoned woodpecker nest hole in a saguaro cactus. Avoiding the sun would help you conserve your body's water supply.
- you would hunt at night when it is cooler. You wouldn't have to drink because you would get all the water you needed from the bodies of the insects and spiders that you ate.

Drink up

Getting a drink of water may be easy for you, but what if you had to reach down more than 4 m (13 ft.), like a giraffe, or could use only your tongue, like a lion? During the dry season on Africa's plains, thousands of animals migrate in search of water. A watering hole is a very busy spot, especially at dawn and dusk. Lions come to drink as well as to hunt. When a lion arrives, the other animals scatter. Check out the animals at this watering hole and find out how they manage to quench their thirst.

Elephant

Flamingo

Like most birds, a flamingo must tip its head back when it takes a drink so that the water flows down its throat.

An elephant's 2 m (7 ft.) long trunk is an extension of its nose and upper lip. The trunk sucks up to 4 L (1 gal.) of water into the animal's mouth.

A lion's tongue is as rough as sandpaper. Water catches on the tongue and is carried into the lion's mouth when it drinks.

Lion

Giraffe

Jackal

In order to reach the water, a giraffe has to spread its front legs out wide and lower itself down slowly. This position makes it hard to escape quickly in case of danger.

Like members of the dog family, a jackal laps up water by curling the end of its tongue to form a cup and lifting the water into its mouth.

35

A liquid diet

For some animals, drinking is not just a way of getting water, it is also how they get their food. When a spider catches a fly in its web, the spider doesn't actually eat the fly. Instead, it drinks the fluids from the fly's body. Vampire bats are famous for their diet of blood. Using their tiny, sharp teeth, vampire bats make a small cut in a mammal's or a bird's skin and lap up the flowing blood with their tongue. This lamprey is well adapted for its role of feeding on the blood of other fish.

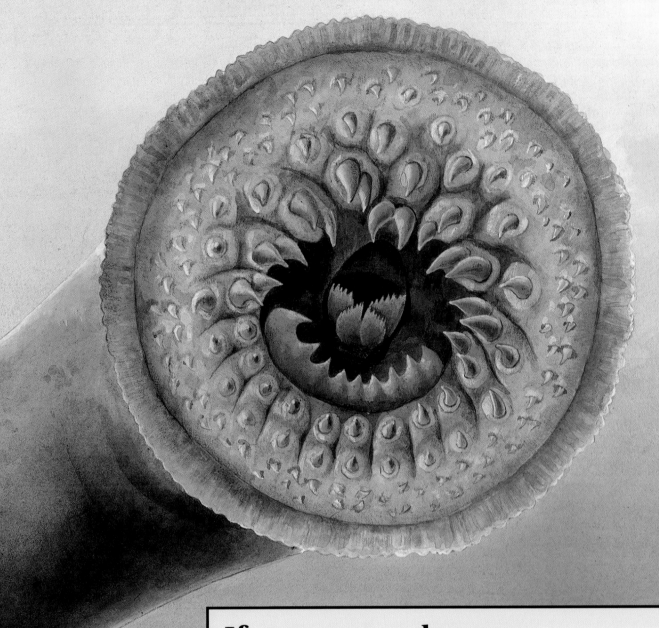

If you were a lamprey ...

- you wouldn't have any jaws. Instead you would have a round, sucking mouth that could cling to your prey.
- your mouth would have as many as 125 sharp teeth. You would work your teeth back and forth until they drilled a hole into your prey's body.
- glands inside your mouth would produce a liquid that would keep the prey's blood flowing.
- you wouldn't kill your prey, but you would weaken it. Fish often die later after several lamprey attacks.

Something sweet

Kids aren't the only ones who like a sweet treat. Many plants are pollinated by bats, insects and hummingbirds that are attracted to a flower by its sweet nectar. Nectar-feeding bats and hummingbirds both have long tongues to help them reach down inside a flower to lap up its nectar. They can also hover in the air over the flower they are feeding on. This helps the animals approach a flower from any angle and feed without landing on the flower, which could break.

Sapsuckers feed on sweet liquid, too, but instead of going after a flower's nectar, they lap up tree sap. Like other woodpeckers, sapsuckers use their hard, pointed beaks to make holes in the trunks of trees. The holes fill with the tree's sweet sap and the birds lick it up with their long tongues.

Sapsucker

Hummingbird

Long-nosed bat

Straws and sponges

Try this activity to see how two different insects, a butterfly and a housefly, feed on liquids.

You'll need:

two saucers

sugar

water

a straw

a sponge

a spoon

1. Put some sugar in one saucer and pour some water into the other saucer.

2. Suck up some water from the saucer with the straw. Part of a butterfly's mouthparts are joined together to make a strawlike tube for sucking nectar out of flowers. When a butterfly is finished feeding, its tongue rolls back up under its head. The scent of nectar makes the tongue stiffen out into a strawlike tube again.

3. Dip a dry sponge into the sugar. Some sugar may cling to the outside of the sponge, but it is not absorbed into the sponge. Now add some of the water to the sugar and stir it until the sugar dissolves. Dip the sponge into the sugar solution. This time the sponge will absorb some sugar along with some water. A fly's lower lip is like a sponge and it can eat only liquid food. When a fly lands on something sweet, like sugar, it cannot eat the sugar in its solid form. First the fly spits on the food to dissolve the sugar with its saliva. Then the fly soaks up the sugar solution with its spongelike mouth.

Index

Answers

Tell the tooth, page 15

1 - C. carnivore (wolf)
2 - A. rodent (porcupine)
3 - D. omnivore (human)
4 - E. herbivore (deer)

Whose hoard?, page 31

Red squirrel - Mushrooms
Mole - Earthworms
Honey bee - Honeycomb
Honeypot ant - Storage ants
Leopard - Antelope
Pika - Mini haystack of
    collected grasses